big
brands

SAMSUNG

Cath Senker

contents

A global brand – Samsung today **4**

Samsung starts out **6**

The global arena **8**

A new management style **10**

Creating a market for electronics **12**

Building the Samsung brand **14**

Samsung v Sony **16**

18 Overcoming recession and scandal

20 Sponsorship

22 The consumer culture

24 The secrets of Samsung's success

26 Samsung's future

28 Market a new Samsung product

30 Glossary and Further information

32 Index

A global brand:
Samsung today

Have you looked in a phone shop recently? If you glanced at the latest smartphones, you probably spotted a few Samsungs.

The Samsung Galaxy S, one of the company's high-end smartphones.

The brand is well known for its classy mobiles – in 2013, one-third of smartphones bought worldwide were Samsungs! Samsung has introduced us to futuristic devices, such as the ultra-high-definition TV with its curved screen, and the Gear S Smartwatch, a slim, wearable smartphone with a keyboard, navigation system, music player and personal fitness monitor. Samsung leads the world in the development of graphene, the super-thin touchscreen material of the future.

In 2014 Samsung was the world's largest electronics and information technology (IT) company for the fourth year running. As well as smartphones, it makes all kinds of electronics and components, including TVs and memory chips. Based in South Korea, the company is also involved in skyscraper and plant construction, fashion, medicine, finance, and the petrochemical and hotel industries. In 2013, its revenue reached around US $216 billion (£135 billion) – more than rival tech companies HP, Siemens and Apple.

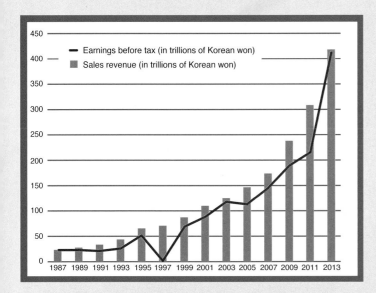

In 2013 Samsung was ranked eighth in Interbrand's list of the world's most valuable brands. Samsung's excellent product designs are key to its success; it won nine design awards in 2013. The brand is also known for new innovations – it has clocked up some world 'firsts', such as WiBro, the first mobile broadband technology. Because the brand is so powerful, Samsung is able to charge premium prices. It sells its TVs, mobiles and memory chips at higher prices than most of its competitors.

This book looks at how Samsung developed from a South Korean manufacturer of sugar, wool and chemicals to become one of the top global electronics companies. What allowed it to become the market leader in producing memory chips? How did it overtake its rival Sony, and manage to create smartphones to rival Apple's best-selling iPhones? What enables it to stay ahead of its competitors and how likely is it to remain at the top of the fiercely competitive electronics market?

Business Matters
Brand value

Indications of brand value include how well branded products sell, and the role of the brand in the decision to buy them.

The Samsung Gear S smartwatch lets you use your phone hands-free.

Samsung starts out

In the early years, Samsung sold groceries.

Samsung was founded as a food export company by ambitious Korean business-man Byung-Chull Lee in 1938. In the mid-1950s, after the Korean War (1950–53) left the country divided into North and South Korea, Samsung became a major corporation. It manufactured sugar, flour, woollen fabric and chemical fibres, and sold financial services. In 1961, a military (army-run) government took power in South Korea. It supported Samsung's growth because it was good for building up the poor economy. Byung-Chull became the richest man in South Korea.

orking at the
amsung Electronics
ctory in the 1980s.

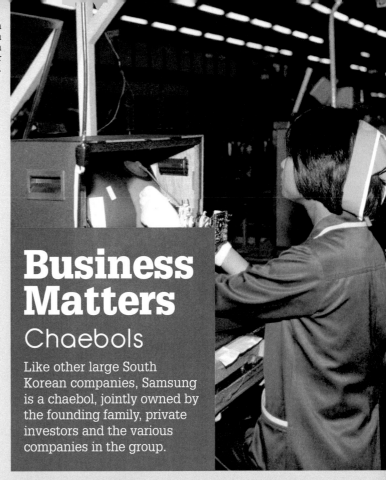

Byung-Chull Lee

Founder of Samsung

Byung-Chull Lee founded Samsung on the Japanese model. As Chief Executive Officer (CEO), he was the 'father' of the company, the employees were his 'family', and there was harmony between them. Workers had a job for life and the longer they worked for the company, the higher their salary. This management model was later adapted to better suit the changing business environment.

Business Matters

Chaebols

Like other large South Korean companies, Samsung is a chaebol, jointly owned by the founding family, private investors and the various companies in the group.

In 1969 Byung-Chull Lee moved into the expanding electronics industry, founding Samsung Electronics and Sanyo-Samsung Electronics as part of the Samsung Group. Much of the technology, including the components, came from Japan, but from 1973–4, oil prices quadrupled, damaging economies worldwide. Japan cut back much of its investment in Korea.

Byung-Chull decided Samsung would manufacture its own components and took over Korea Semiconductor, which produced silicon chips. (There are two kinds of chips: the microprocessor, which has the instructions for computer programs, and the memory chip, which holds programs and information.) Samsung made great strides in the industry, and in 1983 developed a high-speed memory chip. By now, it was South Korea's top company.

> **Samsung's research lab… reminded me of a dilapidated [run-down] high-school science classroom. But the work going on there intrigued me. They'd gather color televisions from every major company in the world… and were using them to design a model of their own.**
>
> **Ira Magaziner, a US business consultant who visited Samsung Electronics in 1977**

the global arena

In 1987, the military government in South Korea finally came to an end. Under the new government, people became better off, and were eager to buy Samsung TVs, video recorders and washing machines. Samsung also developed chemical, genetic engineering and aircraft industries.

Kun-Hee Lee, who took over as Samsung's chairman in 1987, was not content with owning South Korea's biggest company; he wanted Samsung to be a global leader. To rise to the challenge, he attempted to change the management style, encouraging young staff to join and to develop their own ideas. But senior managers who had worked at Samsung for many years resisted change. They wanted the juniors to obey instructions, and were obsessed with increasing sales rather than developing new products.

Kun-Hee decided on a fresh approach. Samsung would focus on its semiconductor industry, which required huge investment in equipment, technology and expert staff. It presented an ideal opportunity to shift the way the business operated. In 1992, Samsung Electronics achieved its first important success, becoming the world's leading company in semiconductors. It developed the world's first 64MB DRAM, the most common form of random access memory (RAM) for computers.

Chairman Kun-Hee Lee focused on company strategy and left day-to-day decisions to his managers.

Samsung Aerospace was involved in the development of Lockheed Martin's F-16 fighter aircraft from 1997 to 2004.

Yet the Samsung Group's home appliances weren't doing as well. They achieved high sales in South Korea, but were not in the first rank globally. In 1993, Kun-Hee watched a programme on Samsung's in-house TV network and was appalled to see workers sawing washing machine lids by hand to make them fit properly. The products simply weren't good enough.

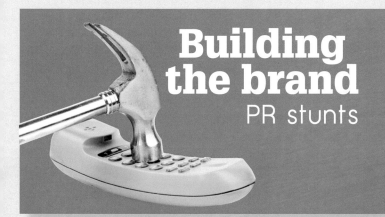

Building the brand
PR stunts

A dramatic PR stunt can draw attention to a business and change its image. In 1995, Samsung gave 2,000 cordless phones to its employees as a New Year gift. When many complained about the poor quality of the devices, Kun-Hee was furious. He asked them to bring back the phones, and recalled poor-quality car phones and fax machines too. Workers at the Samsung factory in Gumi, wearing headbands saying 'Ensure quality', smashed up the faulty goods and set fire to them. This was Kun-Hee's message to the world that Samsung was determined to do better.

Jong-Yong Yun
Samsung Electronics Chief Executive Officer (CEO), 1996–2008

Jong-Yong Yun steered Samsung through its most difficult decade. In 1998, he cut the company's debt by US $13 billion (£8 billion) in one year by selling off failing businesses, made operations more efficient and cut costs. Jong-Yong Yun pushed for Samsung to embrace digital technology and produce high-quality consumer electronics, such as mobile phones. He encouraged improved communications among the workforce by giving all staff notebook computers and mobiles.

a new management style

In 1993, Chairman Kun-Hee revealed his New Management Initiative to make Samsung a dominant global company. He switched the company's focus from the quantity to the quality of the goods produced.

A worker carrying a placard bearing the face of Kun-Hee Lee at a protest about job losses at Samsung in 1998.

Kun-Hee introduced elements of the US business model. Staff now earned a salary based on their performance, rather than how long they had worked for Samsung. Instead of vertical communication alone, from managers down to juniors, he encouraged horizontal communications among skilled workers at the same level. Everyone had to believe 'change begins with me'. Kun-Hee also fostered a sense of crisis to keep everyone on their toes, foretelling that 'All of Samsung's number-one products will disappear in 5 or 10 years'. He pushed the company to adapt to change.

In 1997, an economic crisis hit East Asia. Samsung sold off unprofitable businesses and cut the workforce, which was considered a very 'un-Korean' thing to do. Yet to push the business forward, it offered generous salaries to talented new staff, often from abroad.

A worker at Samsung's factory in Cikarang, Indonesia in 2006.

Samsung made huge investments in the research and development (R&D) of new products, picking areas that it hoped would be popular – mobiles, flat-panel computer monitors and memory chips. The company had been behind in producing analogue devices but now it focused on new digital technologies. Entering the digital technology market early enabled the company to get ahead of its competitors. Overall, the strategy was successful, and Samsung emerged stronger than ever.

Business Matters

Research and development (R&D)

Companies carry out R&D to find new products and processes or to improve existing ones.

> **My co-workers spend a lot of time discussing each other's ideas to help each other develop them further.**
>
> Wesley Park, Samsung manager, 2005

	Samsung's growth stages		Major events at Samsung
1938– mid-1950s	Foundation and establishment of Samsung's management system	Small and middle-sized company (foundation and formation of core businesses)	Entry into manufacturing (1953–1954)
Mid-1950s– late 1960s	Growth into a large company	Large company (initial stage as a business group)	Diversification (electronics, heavy industry and chemicals)
Late 1960s– late 1980s	Emerges as S. Korea's leading company	Large business group	Start of the semiconductor business
Late 1980s– present	Emerges as a world-class company	Global business group	New Management initiative (1993) Restructuring (late 1990s) Global number-one products (in electronics, shipbuilding, heavy industry and chemicals)

Building the brand
Investing in manufacturing

Electronics companies succeeded in creating a market for their products. But there were many competing companies. How did Samsung stay ahead of the game? It developed the lead in a specialist area: memory chips. Samsung's huge investment in manufacturing facilities for memory chips allowed it to widen the gap with its rivals. Whatever new products were developed, they would require chips, and Samsung was the world leader, able to produce them in massive quantities.

In 1999, workers in a factory near Seoul make Samsung's latest product, the notebook computer.

deo recorders (VCRs) are
sembled at Samsung Electronics in
90. VCRs allowed people to record
programmes, a new innovation.

Creating a market for electronics

A big challenge for companies producing goods using new technologies is creating a market for them. In the late 20th century, how did Samsung and other electronics companies persuade people to buy products they had never needed before?

Timing was key. Samsung Electronics was set up at the perfect moment. The supply of electricity was growing in South Korea in 1969. Koreans saw that people in the West had TVs, fridges and fans, and they wanted them too. Samsung successfully exploited the availability of electricity to provide products that used it.

Likewise, Samsung's move into producing the semiconductors used in microprocessors was well timed. The development of microprocessors enabled computers to be made much smaller, in larger quantities and far more cheaply than before. In the 1980s, these personal computers (PCs) were marketed to businesses. Companies such as Microsoft created software applications for businesses, including word-processing programs and spreadsheets for doing accounts. Bill Gates, the co-founder of Microsoft, talked of a future where there would be 'a computer on every desk'. This prediction proved true, and soon computers were an essential business tool.

From the mid-1990s, the Internet took off in wealthy countries, and now people wanted to have PCs for entertainment as well as work. The price of computers fell further, and electronics companies pushed for everyone to have a computer at home. At this time, Samsung was a main supplier of computer components.

Business Matters
Advertising

When companies develop new technologies, they invest heavily in advertising to sell them. Computer companies were extraordinarily successful; the number of computers sold rose from 50,000 in 1975 to 134.7 million in 2000.

Computers have transformed publishing: here, old books are scanned so that people can read them on a website.

Samsung's stand at a trade fair
Las Vegas promotes the world's fir
curved Ultra High Definition TV

building the Samsung brand

A visitor examines Samsung's brand-new flat-screen monitor at a trade show in the USA, 1996.

C hairman Kun-Hee was determined to push the Samsung brand to the top. From the 1990s, he planned a global marketing campaign to make Samsung a household name in the West.

Samsung switched from making functional basics to focusing on high-value goods – items that consumers wanted on an emotional level. From 1995, it created desirable mobiles and flat-panel LCDs, which were lighter and more energy efficient than the older screens. This was Samsung's new premium-brand strategy. Would it work?

Samsung's head of marketing, Eric Kim, ran a test campaign in the USA in 2001, followed by a huge global marketing campaign. The company broke links with discount stores such as Wal-Mart in the USA and made new alliances with high-end independent stores, such as Best Buy and Sears. Customers started linking Samsung with quality goods. The company also tapped into the appeal of convergence products – devices with many electronic functions, such as colour LCD mobiles and wireless handheld PCs. These moves succeeded in changing Samsung's image from an unfashionable South Korean brand to a popular company producing must-have items to rival Apple's sleek computers and iPods.

Building the brand
Price skimming

From 2001, Samsung decided to go for a policy of price skimming – setting a relatively high price to boost profits. Well-known businesses frequently do this when they launch a new, premium-quality product. If consumers want the latest model, they'll be prepared to pay the price.

> **It was a change in 1996 by our chairman, who wanted to build a brand, not just a product... We looked to the future to build the Samsung brand as iconic – one that everybody would want to have.**
>
> Gregory Lee, Global Chief of Marketing, 2005

Business Matters
Economy pricing

If you sell a product at a low price, more people may be eager to buy it; however, they may also think it's a poor-quality item. Also, you will make less profit per product sold and have less money to invest in the company.

Samsung

Samsung opted to raise its brand image by going head to head with its major competitor, Sony. In 2000, Japanese company Sony was Samsung's biggest rival in DRAMs, electronic appliances and mobiles. Founded around the same time as Samsung, Sony was near the top of the electronics league; only Matsushita and Philips had higher sales. In 2000, its sales were US $70 billion (£44 billion) – more than double Samsung's US $28 billion (£17 billion). But Sony's growth had slowed to 5% per year while Samsung was expanding at a super-fast 25%.

In 2001, Eric Kim announced Samsung intended to overtake Sony within five years, and his goal hit the headlines around the world. The battle was on!

Eric Kim achieved his aim for Samsung to beat Sony within five years; he then resigned to take up a less stressful job.

Business Matters

The benefits of growth

Growth has two main advantages. A large company can buy materials in bulk for a low price. It can also spread costs such as marketing over the whole business – these are called 'economies of scale'.

Sony

South Koreans are extremely hard workers, and the contest with Sony inspired workers at Samsung's main Suwon campus to work harder than ever. As well as mobiles, Samsung created portable DVD players and high-definition-ready LCD TVs – items that consumers bought because they were enticing rather than essential. Its products flew out of the shops. Market experts commented that by 2003, 'young consumers were ogling Samsung cell phones [mobiles] and flat-panel TVs the way their parents once lusted after Sony products'. Two years later, in 2005, Samsung had a higher brand value than Sony.

However, in 2007, business growth worldwide slowed down. Samsung's fantastic growth rate faltered and profits fell. The company faced a fresh crisis.

Eric Kim
Head of Global Marketing, 1999–2004

Korean-American Eric Kim pushed for Samsung to sell products at a higher price. The contest with Sony was also his brainchild. In 2001, Kim came up with the DigitAll campaign. At that time, people in most countries believed that digital technology was just for wealthy users. Kim stressed that Samsung's digital technology could meet everyone's needs – both business and personal – and that investing in its products was worthwhile. This was already true in South Korea, where most people had advanced digital mobiles and internet broadband access was the highest in the world. But it was a revolutionary idea in the USA.

overcoming recession &

Samsung Everland: the company survived the scandal, and in 2014, it was announced it was going to go public – allowing people outside the company to buy shares.

Business Matters
Relocation

Wages are an enormous expense for every company. To cut costs, multinational companies frequently move their factories to countries where wages are lower; in Vietnam in 2007, workers earned around one-tenth of the pay of South Korean workers.

scandal

Samsung lost no time in adopting measures to survive the economic crisis. In 2007, Kun-Hee Lee announced restructuring (company reorganization) and cost-cutting plans. The company moved its main mobile production facilities from South Korea to Vietnam, where labour costs were much lower.

Samsung was hit by another crisis in 2008 – a political scandal. Kun-Hee Lee had begun to transfer his wealth to his son, Jae-Yong Lee, who was a major shareholder in Samsung Everland, South Korea's largest amusement park. In 2007, two directors of Everland were convicted for corrupt practices. They had sold Everland shares to Jae-Yong Lee at less than half the market value (which was illegal). The case damaged Samsung's good reputation, and Kun-Hee was forced to resign. However, he became chairman again two years later.

Samsung overcame this scandal, and the company survived and thrived during the 2008 global economic crisis. Its market share of mobile handsets rose from 16 to 21 per cent in one year, and it grabbed market share from Nokia and Sony Ericsson, keeping its high position despite the introduction of Apple's extremely popular iPhone in 2008. Samsung maintained its lead in producing components, and was a brand that people wanted to own. It focused on its digital convergence strategy – integrating voice, text and images on one device. For example, the 2012 Galaxy camera had a wireless connection so people could instantly upload their photos to share.

Building the brand
Diversification – widening the product range

Big businesses prefer to spread their risks. Realizing that the electronics industry might not continue to prove profitable, Kun-Hee sought new avenues for business in the 2010s. Samsung diversified into new industries, including biotechnology, pharmaceuticals and medical equipment, and invested heavily in biosimilars, which are cheaper versions of brand-name biotechnology drugs. The company does nothing by halves; it aimed to become the principal pharmaceutical company in the world!

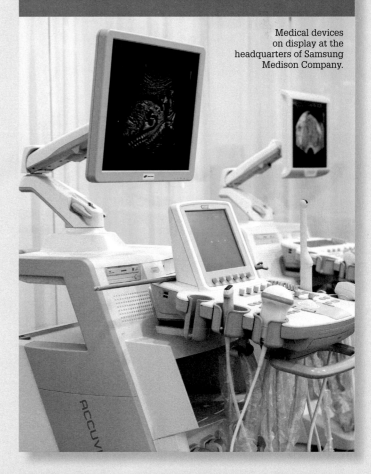

Medical devices on display at the headquarters of Samsung Medison Company.

Sponsorship

The Samsung Olympic Games sponsor lorry accompanies the Olympic torch relay through the British streets.

Top companies queue up to sponsor popular sports competitions to raise the profile of their business and encourage people to link their brand with these exciting events.

From 1998, Samsung became the official sponsor of communications equipment for the Olympic Games, providing wireless communications. Using the Olympics global brand proved ideal for pushing the company worldwide. After the Sydney Olympic Games in 2000, Samsung was placed second in the world after Coca-Cola in brand awareness ranking.

From 2006, Samsung sponsored the Paralympics to build its brand image, as well as other sports. It secured a deal to sponsor the shirts for English football team Chelsea from 2012–15 – every shirt worn by a team member or fan had the name Samsung emblazoned large on the front.

Samsung uses adverts based on Olympics themes in many markets around the world. For London 2012, football star David Beckham was the face of Samsung's Olympics advertising campaign, Everyone's Olympic Games. It spread the message that TV was no longer the main way to enjoy the Olympics. People could watch the games and share their favourite moments immediately on their new Samsung Galaxy phone, with special mobile apps that allowed them to play 3D and augmented reality sports games with their friends.

Business Matters

Building brand affection

Companies look for ways to contribute to society to build affection for their brand. In 2014, Samsung funded the TV programme Launching People in several countries. This recruited celebrities from the food, film, music and photography worlds to mentor budding cooks, film directors, photographers and musicians. The programme featured Samsung tablets, phones and cameras and aimed to show how Samsung technology could help talented people to achieve their dreams.

The launch of Everyone's Olympics Games in London, with David Beckham and athlete Zara Phillips.

> " Consumers are spending about eight minutes per visit on average on 'How Olympic Are You?'. This is double the time they spend on ordinary Samsung sites. "
>
> Ralph Santana, Samsung's Chief Marketing Officer, notes the popularity of Samsung's Olympics-themed webpages in 2012.

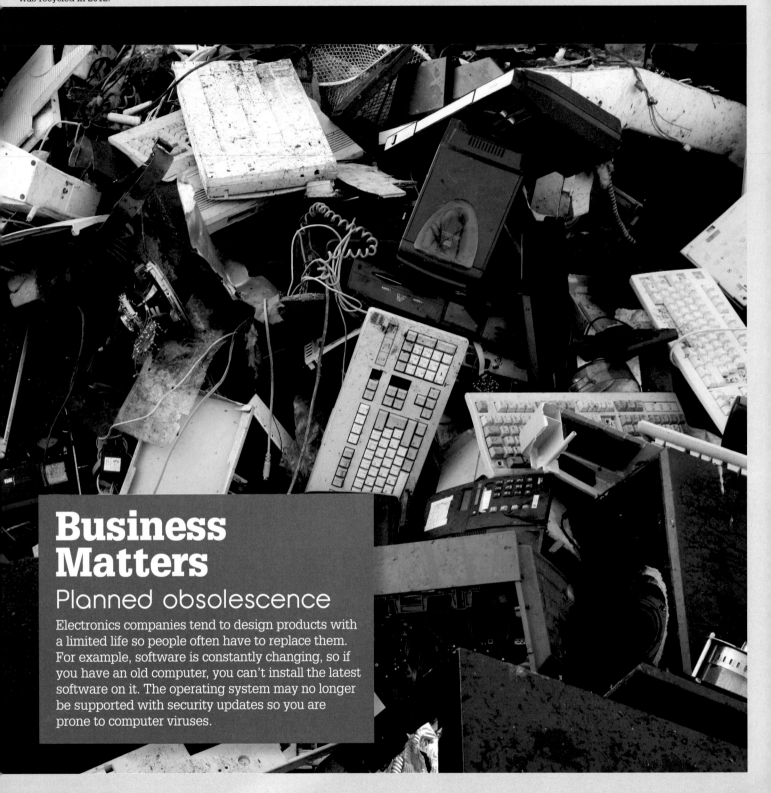

Electronic scrap at a recycling yard. In the USA, just 29 per cent of electronic waste was recycled in 2012.

Business Matters

Planned obsolescence

Electronics companies tend to design products with a limited life so people often have to replace them. For example, software is constantly changing, so if you have an old computer, you can't install the latest software on it. The operating system may no longer be supported with security updates so you are prone to computer viruses.

the consumer culture

Singer, and Samsung ambassador, Lily Allen.

Building the brand
Targeting the youth market

In 2014, Samsung targeted the youth market for mobiles in the UK, using singer Lily Allen to market its new premium handset, the Galaxy Alpha. It aimed to show the smartphone being used by what it called 'Alpha Britons'. According to Samsung, these were young people who 'embody the spirit of new modern Britain and its stylish youth culture.' The marketing campaign was timed to compete with Apple's iPhone 6, which was released at the same time.

Do you really need a new phone each time an upgrade comes out? Mobiles have become a vital accessory, and electronics companies have persuaded many people that it's best to have the newest version with the latest features.

Businesses use social media networks to entice consumers to purchase new products. Samsung has had huge success on Facebook, promoting its major product launches to reach 25 million fans in Europe in 2013. As well as providing information about its devices, it promotes two-way communication with fans, who can share their stories about Samsung purchases. This enables the company to pick up on any problems with its new releases and address them quickly.

The culture of constantly renewing our electronic gadgets has a cost to the environment though – we create mountains of electronic waste, much of it containing toxic materials. Many materials can be reclaimed and recycled, but this takes money and resources. Samsung is trying to clean up its act. In 2012, it was 7th in the Greenpeace Guide to Greener Electronics. It is a leader in providing warranties and spare parts information to help extend product lifetimes. Yet few people use their gadgets for the full lifespan.

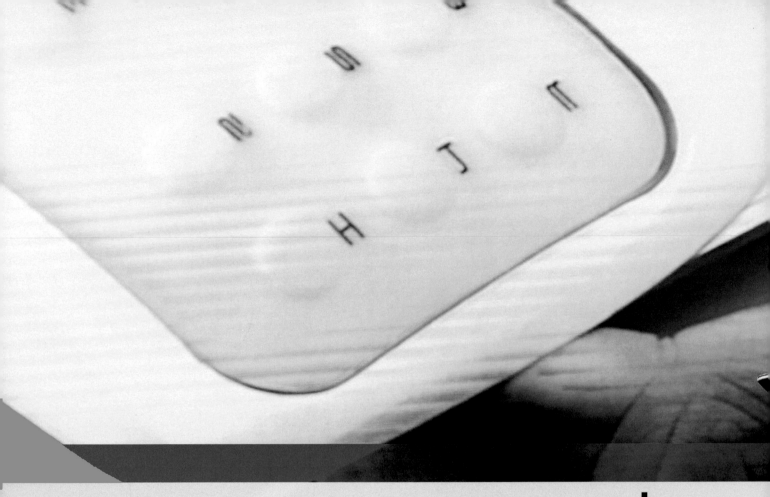

the secrets of Samsung's success

The Samsung booth at an electronics show in Las Vegas, USA in 2014.

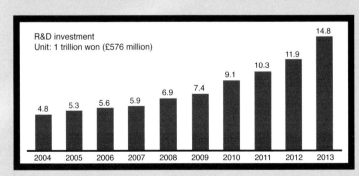

R&D investment
Unit: 1 trillion won (£576 million)

2004	2005	2006	2007	2008	2009	2010	2011	2012	2013
4.8	5.3	5.6	5.9	6.9	7.4	9.1	10.3	11.9	14.8

Business Matters

Co-opetition

Samsung has coined the term 'co-opetition' – a mixture of competition and cooperation – to describe how it expects its employees to work. Businesses within the Samsung Group have to compete to outperform each other and compete with outside suppliers to deliver parts and materials. Yet each division has to create innovative products, so employees have to cooperate together within their teams.

How does Samsung stay ahead of its competitors? In Korea, ppali ppali (quickly, quickly) is a common saying. Samsung has adopted the ppali ppali spirit, bringing out products faster than its rivals. In the mid-2000s, Japanese companies took an average of ten months to plan and release camera mobiles, while Samsung completed the same process in half the time. The speed of production forms an essential part of the brand's message: if you want the latest innovation, buy Samsung.

The company is able to churn out new products speedily through 'leapfrog' R&D. While it is designing a product, employees are already working on the next-generation, the next-next generation and even the one after that!

Production is fast because Samsung has its division headquarters (control centre), major R&D and manufacturing facilities in South Korean cities that are all within a radius of 30 km (18 miles) of each other. The core parts of the Samsung Galaxy S5 phone are all made within the Samsung Group. Having all the sites close together allows for good communications between the different divisions and a fast decision-making process. Experts from the R&D teams meet with the engineers from the manufacturing plant to discuss production issues, resolve any problems and make changes straight away.

From 2000, Samsung set out to lead the market in innovation – each company and division was expected to create a novel product. To foster creativity, it has Creative Labs (C-Labs) and a Creative Academy to encourage employees to come up with new ideas. On 'C-Lab days', they demonstrate the results of their efforts. It was this drive for bright ideas that led to the development of LED TV and wireless broadband.

Samsung's future

Samsung phones on display in a shop in Thailand.

Nothing is guaranteed in the fast-moving electronics businesses. Even market leaders can sink into crisis. The industry may change, leaving them behind while newcomers enter the market and forge ahead. In 2014, Samsung was faced with slowing demand and increased competition in the smartphone industry, and profits fell. The company needs to innovate constantly to survive. What could Samsung do to keep up its global position?

Samsung hasn't acquired as many other companies as its competitors. To adopt new technologies and products, it could invest more in other companies. A good way to foster innovation is to employ a wide range of employees with different skills. Experts have pointed out that the company increasingly hires more women, young and international workers, but it could do more in this area, and give them more responsibility.

More importantly, Samsung could work towards being a Total Solution Provider, providing customers with integrated (well-linked) systems. It has created excellent products, such as MPEG-4 (a way of making small files for sending video and images), digital TV and IMT-2000 (mobile telecommunication standards for 3G mobile services), all of which were chosen for use worldwide. It introduced Tizen, its own operating system, on smartphones in 2014.

Business Matters
Transnational companies (TNCs)

Samsung is a multinational; it is based in its home country. Transnational companies have all their departments located in the best place, for example, where suitable workers live or costs are low. This may not be its home country. Yet if Samsung became a TNC, it would lose the benefits of having its divisions close together.

However, it hasn't developed its own 'platform products' – groups of software and products that have never been seen before. Apple did this by creating iTunes software and iPod music players. Yet Samsung is good at predicting trends and creating new products quickly. It developed the first graphene semiconductors and has a chance to lead the field with this breakthrough technology that could bring us a brand-new generation of must-have gadgets.

> **By 2020, we seek to achieve annual sales of USD 400 billion while placing Samsung Electronics' overall brand value among the global top 5.**
>
> **Samsung website**

market a new Samsung product

When you create a fantastic new product, you need to come up with a marketing strategy to sell it. Here's a sample marketing strategy for a possible device. Why not see if you can come up with your own idea for a Samsung product?

The Samsung Do-it-all

Building on the DigitAll idea, the Do-it-all combines all the functions of a smartphone, tablet, laptop and camera on a super-thin graphene computer that you can unroll to use wherever you are.

Stage 1 Work out your objectives

Step 1: Make sure they fit with your corporate strategy.
The Do-it-all fits perfectly with Samsung's strategy to be the first to bring out an innovative product.

Step 2: What do you hope to achieve?
Samsung's primary goal is to become the market leader. However, investing in this new technology may not bring in large profits immediately, so there are risks involved.

Stage 2 Product detail

Step 1: Product description and positioning
What is it?
The Do-it-all replaces the need for a separate computer, smartphone and camera. Made from graphene, it can be rolled out to the size of a small laptop with a keyboard, yet is as portable as a mobile. A high-quality camera is included as standard.

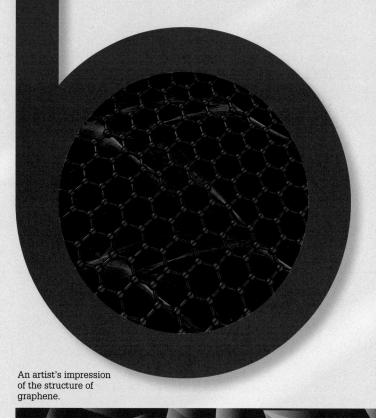

An artist's impression of the structure of graphene.

Who is it for?
People who buy top-end Samsung mobiles and fans with an interest in the latest technology.

How is it different from other products?
There is no computer or smartphone like it. If Samsung brings out the first model, it will have a huge competitive advantage.

What's the benefit?
Convenience and style: you have all your data, photos and videos on one device.

What is the evidence to support your claims?
The Do-it-all will be thoroughly tested for durability to ensure it survives being dropped on the ground, rattling around in bags and falling in water.

Step 2: What will it be used for?
It will have all the functions of laptops, smartphones and digital cameras.

Step 3: How will it be different from other products?
No other product will offer so many functions in such a light format. It will be packaged in a unique case so that it can be carried in its rolled-up form.

Step 4: What is the pricing policy?
Samsung's aim will be to enhance the perception of the brand as a leader in innovation. In keeping with Samsung's general policy, prices will be high to reflect the quality of the product.

Step 5: What's the USP?
It is the first product of its kind.

Stage 3 Understand the market
Step 1: Work out which niche gives the best sales possibilities
At first, this premium-quality, high-priced product will be sold in the wealthiest markets with the most advanced technology, such as Japan, South Korea, the USA, Australasia and Europe.

Step 2: Create customer profiles
Market research will identify target customers by focusing on the profile of people who buy top-end mobiles and laptops, and electronics fans.

Step 3: How will you access customers?
Feature articles will be written for the technology and electronics press and all the social media used by target customers.

Stage 4 Check the competition
What competition is there likely to be?
Other prominent electronics companies such as Google and Apple are likely to produce mobile and wearable graphene devices.

Stage 5 Build your sales plan
Step 1: Key messages
Key messages for the target audience will exploit the desirability of a graphene device on an emotional level – the opportunity to own a product at the forefront of technology – as well as the practicality and convenience of the Do-it-all.

Step 2: Promotion
The promotion strategy will include advertising in the press, TV, cinemas and billboards. Samsung's public relations team will offer information about the Do-it-all. A Do-it-all website and a huge social media and mobile marketing campaign will be set up, and there will be promotions to engage customers, including competitions to win the new device.

Stage 6 Launch!
High-profile launch events involving celebrities will be held in all key target markets, timed for the pre-Christmas period to encourage the highest levels of sales.

glossary

analogue
An electronic process used before digital processing.

application – 'app' for short
A program designed to do a particular job.

biotechnology
The use of living cells and bacteria in industrial and scientific processes.

Chief Executive Officer (CEO)
The person at the top of a business.

component
One of several parts of which something is made.

corrupt
When someone uses their power to do dishonest or illegal things in return for money or to gain an advantage.

digital
An electronic process using a system of receiving and sending information as a series of ones and zeros.

division
A large and important unit or section of an organization.

electronics
Equipment that uses electronic technology, with many small parts, such as microprocessors and memory chips, which control and direct a small electric current.

facility
A place, usually including buildings, used for a particular purpose or activity.

graphene
The strongest, lightest and thinnest material known.

initiative
A new plan for dealing with a problem or achieving a purpose.

innovation
The introduction of new things, ideas or ways of doing something.

investment
Putting money into a business in the hope of making more money.

liquid crystal display (LCD)
A way of showing data in electronic equipment. An electric current is passed through a special liquid, and numbers and letters can be seen on a small screen.

manufacturing
The business or industry of producing goods in large quantities in factories.

marketing
The activity of presenting, advertising and selling a company's products in the best possible way.

memory chip
A chip that holds data. RAM chips hold data temporarily while flash memory chips hold data permanently.

mentor
To advise and train someone with less experience.

microprocessor
A small unit of a computer that has the instructions for computer programs.

operating system
The 'go between' that communicates between the software programs and the hardware (the parts of the computer) to make the computer work.

premium
High quality.

random access memory (RAM)
Computer memory in which data can be changed or removed and can be looked at in any order.

revenue
The money a company earns from the sale of goods and services.

scandal
An event that people think is morally or legally wrong and causes public feelings of shock or anger.

semiconductor
A device containing a solid substance that conducts electricity in particular conditions, used in electronics.

share/shareholder
A company is divided into many equal units called shares. People can buy shares to own part of the company and receive a part of the profits – they are called shareholders.

software
The programs that run on a computer.

sponsor
A company that pays towards a radio or television programme or sporting event, usually in return for advertising.

warranty
A written agreement in which a company selling something promises to repair or replace it if there is a problem within a particular period of time.

How electronics businesses can build their brand

Make sure your customers have a positive experience with your product and address any problems straight away.

Focus on product design, giving your products the same distinctive features, such as the colour, feel and sound.

Have one master brand rather than many separate brands.

Emphasize the benefits that the products bring to people's lives.

Focus your marketing messages on your flagship (top) products.

Deliver your message through the right channels for the target market, depending on the kind of media they access.

Make sure your product names and logos are suitable in different countries.

Check there is a market for your products.

Ensure you can deliver your product reliably to your target market.

A
advertising 13, 20, 29
Apple 4, 5, 14, 19, 23, 27, 29
apps 20

B
biosimilars 19
brand affection 20
brand value 5, 17, 27

C
chaebols 7
convergence products 14
co-opetition 25
Creative Labs (C-Labs) 25

D
digital convergence strategy 19
diversification 19

E
economy pricing 15
environment 23
Everland 18, 19

F
Facebook 23

G
Galaxy 4, 19, 20, 23, 25
graphene 4, 27, 28, 29
growth 6, 16, 17

H
high-value goods 14

I
Interbrand 5

K
Kim, Eric 14, 16, 17

L
Launching People 20
Lee, Byung-Chull 6-7
Lee, Jae-Yong 19
Lee, Kun-Hee 8, 10, 19

M
marketing 14, 15, 17, 23, 29

Matsushita 16
memory chips 4, 5, 7, 11, 12
microprocessors 7, 13

N
Nokia 19

O
Olympics 20-21

P
Philips 16
planned obsolescence 22
ppali ppali 25
price skimming 14
profits 14, 17, 26, 28
public relations (PR) 8, 9, 29

R
relocation 18
research and development (R&D) 11, 24, 25
restructuring 19
revenue 4

S
semiconductors 7, 8, 13, 27
shares 18, 19
silicon chips 7
smartphone 4, 5, 23, 26, 28-29
social media 23, 29
Sony 5, 16-17, 19

T
Tizen 26
Total Solution Provider 26
Transnational Comanys (TNCs) 26

U
ultra high definition TV 4, 14

W
WiBro 5

Y
Yun, Jong-Yung 10

Published in paperback in 2017 by Wayland

Copyright © Hodder & Stoughton, 2017

All rights reserved.
Dewey Number: 338.7'621381-dc23
ISBN: 978 0 7502 9266 5
Ebook ISBN: 978 0 7502 9265 8
10 9 8 7 6 5 4 3 2 1
Printed in China

Wayland
An imprint of Hachette Children's Group
Part of Hodder & Stoughton
Carmelite House
50 Victoria Embankment
London EC4Y 0DZ
An Hachette UK Company
www.hachette.co.uk

www.hachettechildrens.co.uk
Editor: Elizabeth Brent
Designer: Grant Kempster

Picture Credits: Cover: Caro/Photoshot (left), Kobby Dagan / Shutterstock.com (right); p4: Zeynep Demir/Shutterstock.com; p5: Ivan Garcia/Shutterstock.com; p6: Patrick Robert/Sygma/CORBIS (top), Mohumed Maaidh/Wikicommons; p7: Janet Wishnetsky/CORBIS (right); p8: JUNG YEON-JE/AFP/Getty Images; p9: AirTeamImages (top), TakeStockPhotography/Shutterstock.com (bottom); p10: Sean Gallup/Getty Images (top), LEE JAE-WON/AFP/Getty Images (bottom); p11: Dimas Ardian/Getty Images, Stefan Chabluk (bottom); p12: Michel Setboun/Corbis (top), CHOO YOUN-KONG/AFP/Getty Images (bottom); p13: TopFoto/ImageWorks; p14: Gilles Mingasson/Hulton Archive/Getty Images; p15: Kobby Dagan/Shutterstock.com; p16: JUNG YEON-JE/AFP/Getty Images (top), REX/Sipa Press (bottom); p17: Kobby Dagan/Shutterstock.com; p18: Tanjala Gica/Shutterstock.com (top), JUNG YEON-JE/AFP/Getty Images (bottom); p19: SeongJoon Cho/Bloomberg via Getty Images; p20: Kumar Sriskandan/Alamy; p21: Fred Duval/FilmMagic; p22: Helga Esteb/Shutterstock.com; p23 REX/Image Broker; p24: JEON HEON-KYUN/epa/Corbis (top), Kobby Dagan/Shutterstock.com (bottom); p26: Tooykrub/Shutterstock.com, p27: www.exynox.net; p28: LAGUNA DESIGN/Science Photo Library/Corbis

The author would like to acknowledge these sources:
Samsung Electronics and the Struggle for Leadership of the Electronics Industry by Anthony Michell (Wiley, 2010);
The Samsung Way: Transformational Management Strategies from the World Leader in Innovation and Design by Professors Jaeyong Song and Kyungmook Lee (McGraw-Hill, 2014)

The diagrams on pp. 5, 11 and 24 are adapted from *The Samsung Way*.

First published in Great Britain
in 2019 by Wayland
Copyright © Hodder and Stoughton, 2019
All rights reserved

Editor: Amy Pimperton
Text written by Rob Colson and
Jon Richards
Produced by Tall Tree Ltd
Designers: Malcolm Parchment and
Ben Ruocco

HB ISBN: 978 1 5263 0778 1
PB ISBN: 978 1 5263 0779 8

Wayland
An imprint of Hachette Children's Group
Part of Hodder and Stoughton
Carmelite House
50 Victoria Embankment
London EC4Y 0DZ

An Hachette UK Company
www.hachette.co.uk
www.hachettechildrens.co.uk

Printed in China

CONTENTS

WHAT IS LIFE? 4

FASTEST ON THE PLANET 6

SLOW AND STEADY 8

BIG LIVING THINGS......................10

SMALL LIVING THINGS..................12

LONGEST LIVING............................14

LIVING WITH COLD 16

LIVING WITH HEAT........................17

LIVING WITH EXTREMES............18

EXTREME TRAVELLERS................20

EXTREME EATING 22

EXTREME WEAPONS......................24

EXTREME SENSES 26

MOST INTELLIGENT 28

GLOSSARY......................................30

INDEX..32

WHAT IS LIFE?

What makes a living thing actually alive?
Scientists look for seven main characteristics,
or life processes, to decide whether something
is part of the living or non-living world.

MOVEMENT

Living things move, whether this is the sprinting of a
cheetah as it tries to catch its prey, or the slow movement
of a **sunflower** as it tracks the Sun across the sky.

RESPIRATION

Living things produce energy using a chemical reaction called
respiration. This usually involves using **oxygen** and **glucose**
to produce energy, and releases the waste products of
carbon dioxide and **water**.

*When the Sun sets, sunflowers
turn to face east where the Sun
will rise in the morning.*

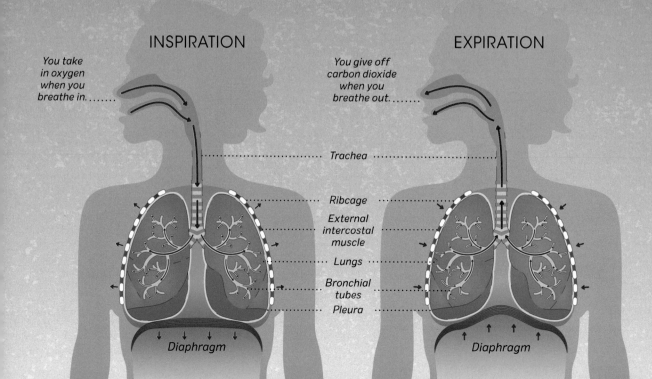

INSPIRATION

*You take
in oxygen
when you
breathe in.*

EXPIRATION

*You give off
carbon dioxide
when you
breathe out.*

Trachea

Ribcage

External
intercostal
muscle

Lungs

Bronchial
tubes

Pleura

Diaphragm

Diaphragm

NUTRITION

Living things need to take in food and nutrients. This could be a **plant** absorbing nutrients from the soil or a **blue whale** swallowing **200,000** tiny **krill** in a single gulp.

Blue whale

Many plants absorb nutrients through their roots.

Krill ....

x200,000

GROWTH

Living things grow up from their juvenile or young phase to maturity. Some animals go through major changes in their body shape and size before reaching maturity. For example, butterflies start off as **eggs**, which hatch into **caterpillars** (pupae), which then go through a **chrysalis** phase, before emerging as an adult **butterfly**.

Eggs are laid on leaves so there is plenty of food when they hatch.

1.

Caterpillars spend nearly all of their time eating.

2.

5

4.

3.

During the chrysalis phase, caterpillars transform into butterflies.

The mature butterfly hatches from the chrysalis.

SENSITIVITY

Living things react to their surroundings. For example, some animals use their **sense** of **sight** to spot dangerous predators.

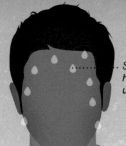

Sweat also helps to cool us down.

EXCRETION

Living things produce waste products that they need to get out of their bodies, such as in **sweat** or **urine**.

REPRODUCTION

Living things create new versions of themselves by reproduction. This can be through asexual reproduction – for example, **bacteria** – where only one individual is involved. Or it can be through sexual reproduction – for example, humans – where one male and one female parent are both involved to produce young.

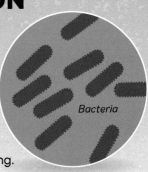

Bacteria

FASTEST ON THE PLANET

These speedy organisms can fly, run, move and swim faster than any other living things on the planet.

FASTEST FLOWERS

Plants may not be known as fast movers, but the **bunchberry dogwood** opens its flowers at record-breaking speed. The petals spring open in just **1 thousandth** of a second (millisecond or ms), catapulting pollen into the air at more than **10 km/h**.

Stage 1: 0 ms

Stage 2: 0.2 ms

Stage 3: 0.4 ms

Stage 4: 1.0 ms

FAST FLIERS

Bats, most birds and some bugs are the only animals that can truly fly, rather than glide. They take to the air by flapping their wings, or using them to catch rising currents of warm air, called thermals.

RAPID REPTILE

Cold-blooded reptiles are not known for their speed, but the fastest lizard, the **bearded dragon**, can escape danger at a brisk **40 km/h**.

The **horsefly** is the fastest insect, and is capable of flying at

145 KM/H

WHITE-THROATED NEEDLETAIL SWIFT
170 KM/H

MEXICAN FREE-TAILED BAT
160 KM/H

A hooked **black marlin** has been recorded pulling line off a fishing reel at a speed equivalent to

132 KM/H.

A falcon's dive is called a stoop.

In a stoop, a peregrine falcon bends back its wings to form a streamlined shape. This reduces friction and drag as the bird passes through the air, maximising its speed.

FASTEST LAND ANIMALS

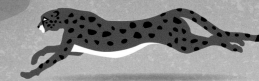

390 KM/H is the speed of a peregrine falcon in a stoop as it swoops down on prey.

Cheetah	120 km/h
Ostrich	97 km/h
Pronghorn	88.5 km/h
Springbok	88 km/h
Lion	80.5 km/h

GOLDEN EAGLE
320 KM/H

... whereas the fastest human runs at just 45 km/h.

SLOW AND STEADY

While some living things rush about from place to place, these organisms like to take their time – and sometimes, being slow and steady will win the race!

ANIMALS IN THE SLOW LANE

Many slow movers live underwater where getting about can be harder, while others move slowly to stay hidden or because they have heavy shells on their backs.

Coral
0 KM/H
Coral is one of the few animals that does not move around.

Sea anemone
0.00008 KM/H
52 days to move 100 metres

Dwarf seahorse
0.02 KM/H
5 hours to move 100 metres

Starfish
0.03 KM/H
3 hours to move 100 metres

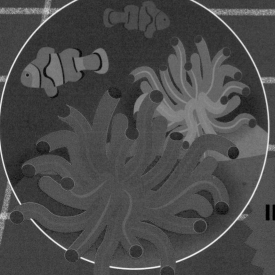

A sea anemone is a predatory

INVERTEBRATE

with no bones. It lives underwater and looks like a plant.

The tentacles of a **sea anemone** contain **venom**, which they use to protect themselves from predators and to kill their prey.

Tortoises move slowly because they do not need to run away from many predators. The thick **armoured shell** on their backs helps protect them from being eaten.

Snails and slugs produce a foul-tasting **slimy trail** that puts off predators.

Slug slime is 'liquid crystal' – neither a liquid nor a solid.

Some slugs are fierce **PREDATORS**.

MOVING MOULD

Slime mould is made up of thousands of tiny **single-celled microorganisms** called **protozoans**. These come together to move slowly across the ground searching for food. They move at about **1 mm per second**, or **0.0036 km/h**, which seems pretty slow, but is actually a speed record for any microorganism.

Mould

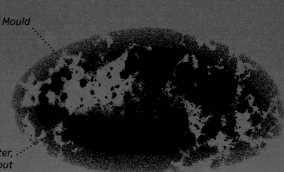

Without water, moulds die, but their spores do not.

Sloths move so slowly that **algae** grows on their fur, turning them **slightly green** in colour, and making them harder to spot among the trees.

Sloth
0.15 KM/H
38 minutes to move 100 metres

Slug
0.3 KM/H
19 minutes to move 100 metres

Giant tortoise
0.3 KM/H
19 minutes to move 100 metres

Garden snail
0.5 KM/H
12 minutes to move 100 metres

Not to scale

BIG LIVING THINGS

The biggest animal that has ever lived is alive today, but millions of years ago, there were gigantic creatures in the seas, the air and on land.

BIGGEST EVER

The **heaviest** animal that has ever lived is the **blue whale**. The water supports the weight of marine animals, which means that they can grow larger. The skeleton of a land animal this size would collapse under the strain!

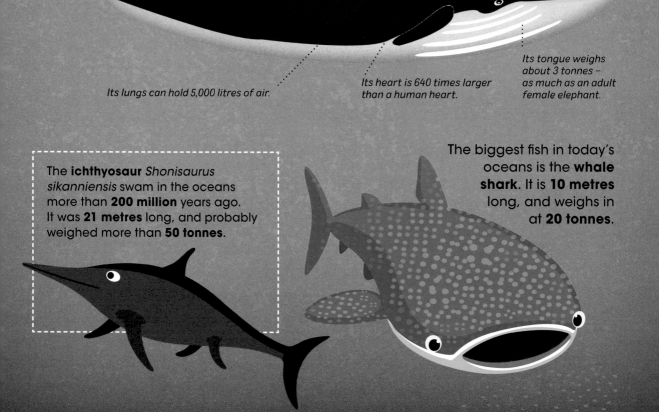

The blue whale is nearly 30 metres long and weighs in at more than 150 tonnes.

10

Its lungs can hold 5,000 litres of air.

Its heart is 640 times larger than a human heart.

Its tongue weighs about 3 tonnes – as much as an adult female elephant.

The **ichthyosaur** *Shonisaurus sikanniensis* swam in the oceans more than **200 million** years ago. It was **21 metres** long, and probably weighed more than **50 tonnes**.

The biggest fish in today's oceans is the **whale shark**. It is **10 metres** long, and weighs in at **20 tonnes**.

IN THE AIR

The biggest prehistoric flying bird was *Pelagornis sandersi*. It had a wingspan of more than **7 metres**. The biggest flying bird today is the **wandering albatross**, with a wingspan of **3.5 metres**.

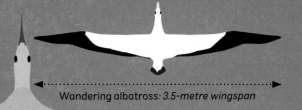

Wandering albatross: 3.5-metre wingspan

Pelagornis sandersi: 7-metre wingspan

The biggest birds are too heavy to fly. The **ostrich** is up to **2.8 metres** tall and weighs **120 kg**. The extinct **giant moa** was **3.6 metres** tall.

3.6 metres

ON LAND

The biggest animals to roam the land were a group of dinosaurs called **sauropods**. The largest of all, *Argentinosaurus*, was nearly 40 metres long and weighed nearly **100 tonnes**.

- The **African elephant** is the biggest land animal alive today. It is up to **4 metres** tall and weighs up to **7 tonnes**.
- The **saltwater crocodile** is the largest living reptile, at **5 metres** long and **1 tonne** in weight.

11

The tallest tree in the world is a **giant redwood** in California, USA, called Hyperion. It stands 115.7 metres tall. That's taller than the **Statue of Liberty**.

92.99 metres

x3 Central Parks

The **Great Barrier Reef** off the coast of Australia is the only living structure that is visible from space. It is **2,300 kilometres** long.

Great Barrier Reef

The largest living thing is a **fungus** called *Armillaria ostoyae*. It grows underground, producing mushrooms at the surface, which are the only sign that it is there. The largest of all, called the **Humongous Fungus**, covers an area of **965 hectares** in Oregon, USA. That's three times the area of Central Park, New York City.

SMALL LIVING THINGS

While huge organisms lumber, soar and power across the planet, these tiny living things can scuttle, swoop and swim unseen from place to place.

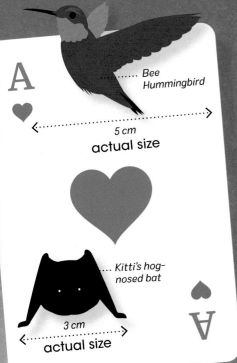

Bee Hummingbird

5 cm
actual size

A

... Kitti's hog-nosed bat

3 cm
actual size

SMALLEST EVER

The smallest bird is the **bee hummingbird**. It is **5 centimetres** long and weighs **2 grams**, about the same weight as a single playing card. It beats its wings 80 times a second, producing a 'humming' sound.

The smallest mammal is the **Kitti's hog-nosed bat**, or **bumblebee bat**, which is **3 centimetres** long and also weighs **2 grams**.

The smallest flower is produced by the plant **Wolffia**, or **duckweed**. It is **0.3** mm across. The plant itself is only the size of a grain of rice.

Sewing needle

......Wolffia

Salt grain

Wolffia seeds

The smallest insect is a **fairyfly** called *Dicopomorpha echmepterygis*. The males are just **0.2 millimetres** long – a little longer than the width of a human hair. They hatch from eggs laid by females inside the eggs of other insects.

The smallest amphibian is the *Paedophryne amauensis* frog, which is just **7.7 millimetres** long. It is also the smallest known vertebrate (an animal with a backbone).

7.7 mm
actual size

.Paedophryne amauensis *frog*

MICROSCOPIC LIFE

Phytoplankton are tiny **single-celled algae** that use energy from the Sun in a process called **photosynthesis**. Like plants, during photosynthesis, they release oxygen into the air. It is estimated that phytoplankton release about **80 per cent** of all the oxygen in the atmosphere. When there are high levels of nutrients in the oceans, phytoplankton can increase rapidly to form huge **algal blooms**.

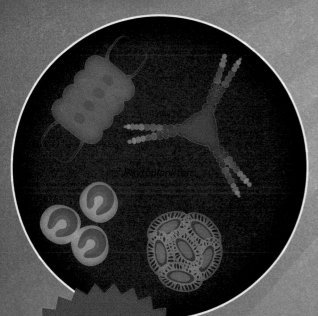

Phytoplankton

Phytoplankton
can form

GIANT
BLOOMS

that are visible
from space.

The phytoplankton are eaten by tiny floating animals called **zooplankton**. These range from single-celled protozoans to crustaceans such as **copepods** and **krill**.

Possibly the smallest living thing is a **bacterium** called *Pelagibacter ubique*, which lives in salt and fresh water. It is less than **1 millionth** of a **metre** (or 1,000 nanometers) long, meaning that more than 100 of them could be placed end to end across a single human hair. As well as being the smallest, it is the most numerous life form. There may be as many as **1,000 trillion trillion** of them, with a total weight greater than that of all the fish in the sea.

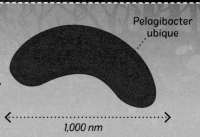

Pelagibacter
ubique

1,000 nm

LONGEST LIVING

Nearly all living things eventually grow old and die. Some may survive for just a few hours, while others can live for hundreds of years. It was once thought that all living things eventually grew old, but there may be some out there that can live forever.

Bowhead whales are named after the distinctive shape of their heads.

ARCTIC VETERANS

The **Greenland shark** is the longest-living vertebrate. It can live for at least **400 years**, and perhaps as long as **500 years**! The secret to its longevity is that it takes life slowly in the cold, deep waters of the Arctic Ocean. It eats little and only grows a few centimetres a year, but can still reach **5 metres** in length. Females do not reproduce until they are at least **150 years old!**

The **bowhead whale** also survives for centuries in the cold Arctic Ocean. The oldest individual discovered by scientists was **211 years** old when it died.

The Greenland shark is one of only two **SHARK** species that can cope with Arctic temperatures all year round.

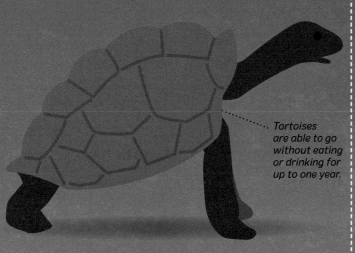

Humans only rarely live beyond **100**. The oldest person whose age was known for certain was a French woman named Jeanne Calment, who died in 1997 at the age of **122 years** and **164 days**.

Tortoises are able to go without eating or drinking for up to one year.

LIFE ON LAND

The oldest land animal ever recorded was an Aldabra giant tortoise called Await. He is thought to have been 255 years old when he died in India in 2006.

Quahog

WHY DIE?

Some aquatic creatures are thought to never age. The **hydra** is a simple animal that lives in fresh water. While the cells of other animals eventually lose their ability to renew themselves, which leads to ageing, studies have shown that the hydra's cells can keep on **reproducing** – and so live – **forever**.

OOPS!

Much like a tree, you can tell the age of a **quahog** (a type of mussel), by counting the growth rings on its shell. *Ming*, the longest-living creature known to scientists, started its life in **1499** and lived for more than **500 years** before it was accidentally killed by scientists in 2006.

Hydras live in lakes, ponds, and slow-moving streams.

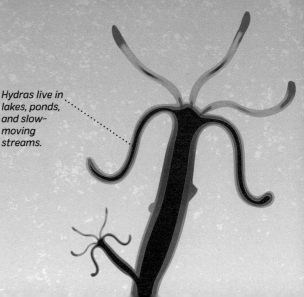

LIVING WITH COLD

Life is tough in the extreme cold and many animals and plants will slow right down to survive a tough winter. Others are so well adapted to the chill that they would die if they were exposed to warmer temperatures.

LIFE IN COLD REGIONS

Wood frogs are found as far north as Alaska, USA. They can survive the cold winters with more than 60 per cent of their body frozen for up to two weeks.

.....Wood frogs live to be 3 to 4 years old.

Red flat dark beetles from Alaska hide under the bark of poplar trees to beat the cold. They can survive temperatures as low as **-150°C**.

Adults are around 3.5 centimetres long.

A **woolly bear moth** spends about **90 per cent** of its caterpillar state in hibernation during the long Arctic winter. During hibernation, its heart and breathing stop completely.

Woolly bear moth

FROZEN FISH

The strange-looking **icefish** lives on the seabed in the Southern Ocean around Antarctica, where the water can be as cold as **-2°C**. Its blood contains a special chemical that acts as an **antifreeze** and stops the fish from freezing.

Icefish

The champion cold survivor is a tiny bacterium called *Chryseobacterium greenlandensis*. This has been known to survive for more than **120,000 years,** frozen solid in an ice block in Greenland.

16

LIVING WITH HEAT

When temperatures soar, these living things have some clever and startling ways of coping with heat.

LIFE IN HOT DESERTS

Sidewinder snakes live in the deserts of southwestern USA and northwestern Mexico. Unlike other snakes, they slither **diagonally**, so just a few parts of their body touch the hot sand.

Thorny devils are lizards found in the hot deserts of Australia. Their bodies are covered in sharp, pointed thorns. As well as protecting them from predators, the thorns collect morning **dew** for the lizard to drink.

Prickly pear cactus

The prickly spines of **cacti** are actually its leaves. The spines **protect** the plant and help to reduce water loss. As a result, the cactus saves a lot of liquid. Extensive **root systems** quickly soak up water during a rare rainstorm.

LIFE IN HOT WATER

Microbes have been found living in the **volcanic springs** in Yellowstone National Park, USA, where temperatures reach **90°C**. Other bacteria have been found living around **hydrothermal vents** on the sea floor, where the plumes of super-hot water can reach **340°C**.

LIVING WITH EXTREMES

Living things have evolved to cope with a variety of extreme conditions, including a lack of water, huge pressure and intense radiation. Some have survived the cold vacuum of space!

Camels store fat in their humps.

DESERT CONDITIONS

Camels can drink more than **100 litres** of water in one go. They store this water in their **bloodstream**, and can go for up to **15 days** without another drink.

Giant kangaroo rats don't drink water at all. Instead, they get all their water from their food.

...... Kangaroo rat

Wide feet stop the camel sinking into the sand

Dung beetles get all their nutrients and water by eating animal poo! They spend hours rolling the poo into balls and then into their burrows. A single ball of poo can keep a dung beetle alive for more than a week.

The **rabbit tobacco plant** grows in the Sonora Desert in North America. Each year, only about **10 per cent** of its seeds **germinate** and start to grow. If they die, more seeds will germinate the next year. In this way, the plant's seeds get several years to have a chance at growing.

Dung ....
beetle

DUNG BEETLES ARE ONE OF THE WORLD'S STRONGEST INSECTS

TOUGH LITTLE CRITTERS

The prize for the toughest living thing goes to the **tardigrade**, or waterbear. These tiny eight-legged water-dwelling animals are just **0.5 millimetres** long. They have been found to survive:

- temperatures as high as **150°C** for a few minutes
- temperatures as low as **-272°C** for a few minutes
- pressures of up to **6,000** times atmospheric pressure
- extreme dehydration – they can survive losing **99 per cent** of their body water.

In 2007, tardigrades were blasted into space and exposed to intense solar radiation for **10 days**. Many were successfully revived when they returned to Earth.

TARDIGRADES ARE ALSO KNOWN AS **MOSS PIGLETS**.

UNDER PRESSURE

The **Mariana Trench** is the deepest place on the planet, reaching nearly **11,000 metres** below the Pacific Ocean. Pressures here are **1,100 times** greater than at sea level. **Amoeba** able to withstand the pressure have been found living at the bottom of this trench. At a depth of **11,000 metres**, a human body would be squashed by the pressure into a sphere the size of a tennis ball!

OTHER DEEP-SEA CREATURES INCLUDE

The **sperm whale** can dive to depths of up to **2,000 metres**. Scientists think that they may be able to collapse their lungs, reinflating them when they rise back to the surface.

The **dumbo octopus**, has been found at depths of more than **4,000 metres**. It has a compact body to survive the pressure, and swims with its two large 'ears'.

Dumbo octopus

DEEP DOWN!

Zombie worms live at **depths** of around **3,000 metres**, feeding on the bodies of dead animals that have sunk to the ocean floor. The worms release acid to burn through the bones to get at the nutrients inside.

EXTREME TRAVELLERS

Some animals travel thousands of kilometres every year in search of food, shelter, or a suitable place to raise their young. Plants and fungi spread across the world by releasing spores or seeds that can travel long distances.

LONG-HAUL FLIGHTS

The champion migrator is the **Arctic tern**. This bird experiences two summers every year – spending six months in the **far north**, then six months in the **far south**.

The arctic tern flies a
70,000-KM
round trip from the Arctic to Antarctica and back again every year.

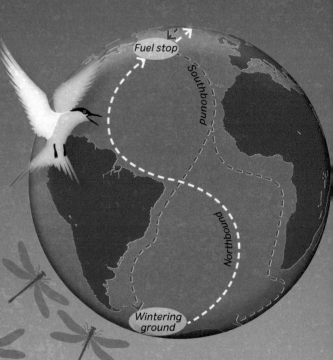

Fuel stop

Southbound

Northbound

Wintering ground

Some insects migrate huge distances in **multi-generational** journeys. The **globe skimmer dragonfly** migrates from India to southern Africa and back – a distance of **18,000 kilometres**, but no individual insect makes the whole journey. The dragonflies that arrive back in India are the great-grandchildren of those that left a year earlier.

LONGEST MIGRATORS

Arctic tern	70,000 km
Sooty shearwater	64,000 km
Common tern	26,000 km
Grey whale	22,000 km
Northern elephant seal	21,000 km
Leatherback turtle	19,300 km
Globe skimmer dragonfly	18,000 km
Bar-tailed godwit	11,000 km
Humpback whale	8,300 km
Tuna	7,700 km

MIGRATIONS ON FOOT

Caribou in the far north of North America are constantly on the move. They walk up to **2,400 kilometres** each year in search of grass to eat between their summer and winter pastures.

Special fur keeps caribou warm. They have thick, woolly fur in winter. During the summer, the fur thins out so the caribou stays cool.

On the grasslands of Africa, huge herds of **wildebeest, zebras** and **gazelles** travel up to **1,000 kilometres** a year in search of fresh grass and water.

AERIAL SPORES

Tiny **spores** are released by fungi into the air, and they can travel right around the world before they find somewhere to develop into a new fungus.

CHAMPION SWIMMERS

Grey whales travel further each year than any other mammal. Each autumn, they embark on a three-month-long journey from the Arctic Ocean to warm waters off Mexico, where the females give birth to their calves. They return north the following spring with their calves in tow – a round trip of up to **22,000 kilometres**.

Leatherback turtles migrate right across the Pacific Ocean each year from their nesting sites in Indonesia to the waters off California, where they feed.

The largest recorded leatherback turtle weighed **916 kg**.

Grey whale

Every day, huge swarms of tiny **plankton** take part in the **biggest mass migration** on the planet. This migration takes place vertically. The plankton come to the surface to feed at night, then sink to the dark depths during the day to avoid being eaten.

EXTREME EATING

If you think you're feeling a little peckish, have a look at what some living things will do to get a decent meal inside them.

BINGE EATING!

Some animals gorge themselves because they don't know when their next meal might be.

Snakes swallow their prey in one go. The biggest snakes, such as **pythons** and **anacondas**, can eat a whole deer. Once swallowed, the food takes anything from a **few days** to **several months** to break down and be digested.

Some snakes can dislocate their jaws to swallow large prey.

Vulture

Vultures can eat **20 per cent** of their body weight in one sitting. Much more than that and they would be too heavy to fly.

Tiger shark

Tasmanian devils can eat **40 per cent** of their body weight in **30 MINUTES**.

Tiger sharks are called the garbage cans of the sea because they will eat anything. The stomachs of some tiger sharks have been found to include **car number plates, tyres and even boots**.

OTHER ANIMALS JUST NEED TO KEEP ON EATING ...

Hummingbirds burn so much energy that they need to eat every **10 minutes**.

Caterpillars have just one job: to eat, day and night. In just a few weeks, they increase their body size **1,000 times** or more before turning into a chrysalis.

Camouflage helps to protect caterpillars from predators.

RICH MILK

Weddell seal mothers produce milk that is **60 per cent fat** and has the **highest calorific** intake of any mammal. This milk helps the baby seals to grow and produce a thick layer of fat, called **blubber**, which keeps them warm in the icy waters around Antarctica.

HUGE QUANTITIES

Giant anteaters in South America use their huge claws to rip open anthills and then poke their long tongues inside to scoop up the ants. In a single day, one anteater can feast on up to **35,000** ants and termites.

Anteater

Venus fly trap

Some plants that live in poor soils **eat meat** to supplement their diet. The **Venus flytrap** lives in wetlands in the eastern USA. It catches insects in special leaves that snap shut when they sense their victims crawling on them.

PLASTIC EATER

Fungi can eat all kinds of things. The fungus *Aspergillus tubingensis* was discovered in a rubbish dump in Pakistan eating the plastic there. Scientists are looking for ways to use fungi to break down our waste.

Blue whales can eat **40 MILLION KRILL (3.5 TONNES)** in a single day!

EXTREME WEAPONS

These living things need a little help in catching something to eat or to avoid being eaten themselves. Fortunately, they have a range of weapons they can use with devastating effects.

ACCURATE WEAPONS!

Banded archerfish can shoot down insects that are up to **3 metres** above the surface of the water, by **spitting** jets of water from their mouths.

Banded archerfish

Horned lizards can change the colour of their skin to **MATCH THEIR SURROUNDINGS** making them almost invisible to any predators.

When threatened, horned lizards can puff up their bodily spines, which make them appear bigger than their actual size.

Horned lizards scare off attackers by **SQUIRTING JETS OF BLOOD** from their eyes up to a distance of 1.5 metres.

Bolas spiders spin a sticky lump of silk, which they hang from the end of a line and swing beneath them to catch any insects flying past.

CLUBS AND SPEARS

Mantis shrimps have one of the most powerful punches around. They can fling out their folded arms at speeds of **80 km/h**. Some species are smashers with blunt **clubs** that they use to crack the shells of snails or crabs. Others have spears, which they use to **harpoon** prey, such as fish.

Mantis shrimp.

With a velocity of 10 m/s, the punch of a mantis shrimp has the power of a .22-CALIBRE BULLET

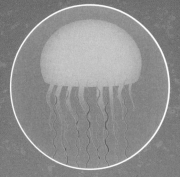

VENOMOUS CREATURES

Box jellyfish are among the world's most venomous animals. The stings of some species can be **fatal** to humans.

SHOCKING

Electric eels can release about **600 volts** of electricity into the water around them to disable and even kill any possible predators. That's about **five** times the power of a socket in the home.

BEETLE ATTACK

Bombardier beetles protect themselves by firing off a **hot**, **noxious spray** from the tip of their abdomen, while also producing a loud **popping** sound. The spray is produced by a chemical reaction between the chemicals **hydroquinone** and **hydrogen peroxide**.

DO NOT EAT!

Many plants and fungi produce poisons to protect themselves against being eaten.

The world's **most poisonous plant** is probably the **castor oil** plant. Its seeds contain deadly **ricin**, and eating as few as four seeds can kill a human.

Toadstools are **poisonous mushrooms**. The **deadly dapperling** is found in woodlands throughout Europe. It damages the liver if eaten, and can be fatal.

Castor bean

EXTREME SENSES

These living things are some of the most sensitive on the planet. They can detect things that are far beyond the abilities of humans.

SUPER VISION

It is hard to sneak up on a **cockroach**, even on a moonless night. Their eyes act like long-exposure cameras, building up a signal over long periods of time to give them enough information to see in pitch-black conditions. They have almost **360-degree** vision, too, so they can see all around them.

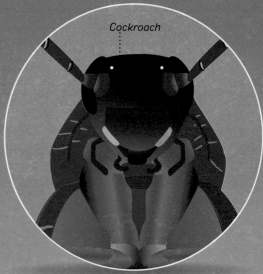

Cockroach

SEEING SOUND

Some animals, such as **bats** and **dolphins**, 'see' the world around them using a sound system called **echolocation**. They give off high-pitched clicks and listen out for the echoes bouncing back off objects around them. It works better underwater than on land because it is easier for sound waves to travel through water than through air.

Reflected echo of fish

Emitted sound of dolphin

Dolphins listen out for the echoes as they bounce off objects to accurately locate their prey.

SEEING HEAT

Vampire bats have special heat-sensitive organs on their heads that detect the infrared light given off by warm prey animals. These sensory organs also help them to identify the hottest part of their prey, where veins carrying blood are closest to the surface of the skin.

MOTH SONAR SENSES

Some species of **moth** have the most sensitive sense of **hearing** in the animal kingdom and are able to hear frequencies up to **300 kilohertz** – that's fifteen times higher than the highest frequency humans can hear.

A catfish's barbels look like a cat's whiskers.

SUPER-SMELLERS

Bloodhounds have super-sensitive snouts. Their noses contain **300 million** scent receptors. A human nose has just **5 million** receptors.

Snakes use their tongues to smell the air. They flick out their **tongues** and catch **scent molecules**. They then flick their tongues into special organs in the roof of the mouth to detect the smells around them.

SUPER-TASTER

Some large **catfish** have **175,000** taste buds – in comparison, humans only have about **10,000**. The taste buds are found all over the fish's body, but concentrated on the four barbels around the mouth, which the fish uses to taste for food in the muddy water, where their eyes are of little use.

Scent molecules are caught on the snake's moist tongue.

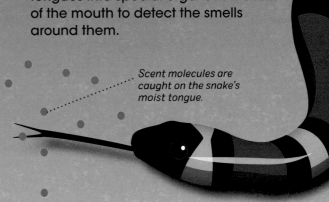

Sensory organs next to bat's nose

Infrared light emitted by warm prey animal

FEELING ITS WAY AROUND

The **star-nosed mole** has an odd-shaped nose with **22 super-sensitive tentacles**. This nose is packed with more than **100,000 nerve endings**, making it one of the most sensitive organs in the animal kingdom. They use their sensitive snouts to detect vibrations and movement of prey in the dark, underground world in which they live.

Star-nosed mole

MOST INTELLIGENT

Which living things are the most intelligent on the planet? You might thing it's us humans, but there are plenty of other clever critters out there and they use their brains to get food, solve problems and communicate with each other.

CLEVER CROWS

New Caledonian crows make tools to help them forage for grubs. They make at least **three different tools** depending on what they want to do with them: **straight sticks, hooked twigs**, and **barbed leaves**. They have strong, short beaks with which to firmly grip their tools.

Barbed leaves Hooked twigs Straight sticks

Some crows **drop nuts** on to roads by pedestrian crossings so that cars run over them and crack them open. The crows wait at the side for the lights to **turn red** before collecting the nuts.

Scrub jays hide food to eat later on. They also steal each other's meals. If a scrub jay notices another bird watching it as it buries its food, it will make sure it **sneaks** back later to move it. Scientists call this 'theory of mind' – a sure sign of cleverness.

Migrating crows
WILL CHANGE
their route to avoid a place where crows have previously been shot.

MAKING TOOLS

Chimpanzees and **bonobos** make and use a range of tools to get food. These include stones to crack nuts and blades of grass to lift termites out of nests. They will also strip twigs to create thin pokers to get at hard-to-reach food.

Octopuses have shown a knack for solving puzzles. When given a **screwed-down jar** with food inside, some will learn how to **unscrew** the jar to get at the tasty treat.

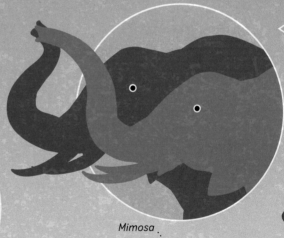

WAGGLE WHILE YOU WORK

Bees perform a '**waggle dance**' to show other bees the direction and distance of sources of nectar. The direction of the dance shows the direction to fly in relation to the Sun, while the length of the dance shows the distance.

Food source

Waggle length indicates distance to food

Light from Sun

Direction to food source

Scout bee

1s = 1km

Scientists believe that **elephants** use a range of gestures and movements, including stroking with trunks, and a range of sounds to communicate with each other.

29

Prairie dogs warn one another that a predator is around, using different barks depending on the species of predator.

Mimosa

PLANT LEARNING

Plants don't have brains, so they cannot think, but some plants have been found to be able to learn, which is a sign of intelligence. *Mimosa pudica*, or the **shy plant**, folds up its leaves to protect itself when it is touched or shaken. It can also learn not to respond to repeated touching that

Leaves fold up

GLOSSARY

ALGAL BLOOM
A rapid growth in the number of tiny marine organisms.

AMOEBA
A single-celled organism that can change its shape, enabling it to move and engulf food.

ASEXUAL REPRODUCTION
The production of young organisms that only involves one parent organism.

ATMOSPHERIC PRESSURE
The pressure caused by the weight of Earth's atmosphere pushing down on a surface.

BACTERIUM
Tiny, single-celled organisms, many of which cause diseases.

BLUBBER
The thick layer of fat found just under the skin of many animals living in cold conditions. This helps to keep the animal warm.

CARBON DIOXIDE
A colourless, odourless gas that is produced by living things during respiration.

CHRYSALIS
The stage in the life cycle of a butterfly or a moth when a caterpillar transforms into the adult butterfly or moth.

COLD-BLOODED
Used to describe an animal that cannot maintain its own body heat. They include insects, reptiles and amphibians.

CRUSTACEANS
A type of animal that has a hard outer shell and several pairs of legs, such as crabs.

ECHOLOCATION
A method of finding objects, including prey, which involves listening to the echoes made as sounds bounce off objects.

EXCRETION
Getting rid of the body's waste products, such as urinating.

FREQUENCY
How quickly something occurs. The frequency of a sound refers to how quickly the sound waves vibrate every second.

FRICTION
The force produced when two materials move over each other.

FUNGUS
A type of living organism. Fungi include mushrooms and toadstools.

GERMINATE
When a living thing begins to grow from a seed or spore.

GLUCOSE
A simple form of sugar, it is used in respiration to produce energy.

HIBERNATION
A sleep-like state that many animals enter during cold periods to preserve energy.

HYDROTHERMAL VENTS
Holes in the sea floor through which super-hot water gushes.

INVERTEBRATE
A type of animal that does not have a spine. Invertebrates include insects and crustaceans.

JUVENILE
The young form of a living thing.

MAMMAL
A type of warm-blooded animal that has a body covered with hair and that produces milk to feed its young.

MATURITY
When a living thing reaches adulthood and its body reaches its fullest extent.

MICROORGANISM
A living thing that is too small to see with the naked eye.

MIGRATION
The regular movement of animals from one region to another.

NOXIOUS
Something that is harmful, poisonous or unpleasant.

OXYGEN
A colourless, odourless gas that is used by living things to produce energy in a process called respiration.

PHOTOSYNTHESIS
The process where plants use sunlight, water and carbon dioxide to produce sugars and oxygen.

PHYTOPLANKTON
The name given to tiny marine organisms that produce energy using photosynthesis.

PUPAE
The stage in an insect's life cycle that comes between a larva and a full-grown adult.

RESPIRATION
The process where living things use oxygen and sugars to release the energy they need to live. This process also produces carbon dioxide and water.

SEXUAL REPRODUCTION
The production of young organisms that involves two parent organisms.

SPORES
Cells produced by bacteria and fungi that will grow into new bacteria or fungi.

ZOOPLANKTON
The name given to tiny marine animals. Zooplankton are mainly young fish and tiny crustaceans.

INDEX

Antarctica 16, 20, 23
anteaters 23
archerfish 24
Arctic tern 20

bacteria 5, 13, 16, 17
bats 6, 12, 26
bearded dragon 6
bees 29
beetles 16, 18, 25
box jellyfish 25

cactus 17
camels 18
camouflage 23
caribou 21
castor oil plant 25
catfish 27
cockroaches 26
cold 14, 16
crows 28
crustaceans 13, 25

deserts 17
dolphins 26
duckweed 12
dung beetles 18

eating 18, 22–23
echolocation 26
electric eels 25
elephants 11, 29
excretion 4

frogs 12, 16
fungi 11, 20, 21, 23, 25

Great Barrier Reef 11
growth 5, 10, 11, 14, 15

heat 17, 26
humans 5, 15
hummingbirds 12, 23
hydra 15
Hyperion 11

ichthyosaur 10
infrared light 26, 27
intelligence 28–29

leatherback turtles 20,
    21
lizards 6, 17, 24

mantis shrimps 25
Mariana Trench 19
marlin 7
microorganisms 9, 17
migration 20–21
moths 16, 27
mould 9
movement 4, 27, 29

octopuses 19, 29
old age 14–15
ostriches 7, 11

peregrine falcon 6-7
photosynthesis 13
phytoplankton 13
plants 5, 6, 13, 16, 17,
    18, 20, 23, 25, 29
poison 9, 25
prairie dogs 29

prehistoric animals 10,
    11

quahog 15

rats 18
reproduction 5
reptiles 6, 11, 15, 17, 24
respiration 4

sea anemones 8, 9
sensitivity 5
sharks 10, 14, 22
sloths 9
slugs 9
smell 27
snails 9, 25
snakes 17, 22, 27
sonar 27
sound 12, 25, 26, 29
speed 6-7, 9
spiders 24

tardigrades 19
taste 27
tortoises 9, 15

venom 9, 25
Venus flytrap 23
vision 26
vultures 22

Weddell seals 23
whales 5, 10, 14, 19, 20,
    21, 23

zombie worms 19

What Can Live in the River?

John-Paul Wilkins

raintree

Raintree is an imprint of Capstone Global Library Limited, a company incorporated in England and Wales having its registered office at 7 Pilgrim Street, London, EC4V 6LB – Registered company number: 6695582

www.raintreepublishers.co.uk
myorders@raintreepublishers.co.uk

Text © Capstone Global Library Limited 2015
First published in hardback in 2014
First published in paperback in 2015
The moral rights of the proprietor have been asserted.

Edited by Diyan Leake and Gina Kammer
Designed by Cynthia Akiyoshi
Picture research by Elizabeth Alexander
and Tracy Cummins
Production by Victoria Fitzgerald
Originated by Capstone Global Library Ltd
Printed and bound in China by Leo Paper Group

ISBN 978 1 406 28497 3 (hardback)
18 17 16 15 14
10 9 8 7 6 5 4 3 2 1

ISBN 978 1 406 28502 4 (paperback)
19 18 17 16 15
10 9 8 7 6 5 4 3 2 1

British Library Cataloguing in Publication Data
A full catalogue record for this book is available from the British Library.

Acknowledgements
We would like to thank the following for permission to reproduce photographs:
Alamy: © AlamyCelebrity/Stefan Hetz Supplied by WENN.com, 19, © Andre Seale, 9, 23f, © blickwinkel, 7, 11, 23a, © Iain Cooper, 5, © Juniors Bildarchiv GmbH, 20, 23h, © Malcolm Schuyl, 10, 23c, © WILDLIFE GmbH, 15, 23d; FLPA: © Terry Whittaker, 8; naturepl.com: © Daniel Heuclin, 22, © Dave Watts, 16, © Jan Hamrsky, 21, © Rolf Nussbaumer, 13; Shutterstock: almgren, 6, BMJ, 7 inset, Bonnie Taylor Barry, 12, back cover right, Kletr, 18, 23e, optimarc, 17, SurangaSL, 4, 23b, back cover left, tim elliott, 14, 23g; Superstock: Ron Erwin/All Canada Photos, front cover.

We would like to thank Michael Bright for his invaluable help in the preparation of this book.

Every effort has been made to contact copyright holders of material reproduced in this book. Any omissions will be rectified in subsequent printings if notice is given to the publisher.

Contents

What is a river habitat?. 4

How do plants live in rivers? 6

How do animals feed
    in rivers? 10

How do animals hide in rivers? 14

How do animals move around
    in rivers? 16

How do animals survive
    under water? 18

How do animal babies survive
    in rivers? 20

That's amazing!. 22

Picture glossary. 23

Find out more 24

Index 24

Some words are shown in bold, **like this**. You can find out what they mean by looking in the glossary.

What is a river habitat?

A **habitat** is a place where animals or plants live. A river is a habitat.

Habitats provide food and **shelter** for the things that live there.

A river is a large stream of water that flows across land.

Animals and plants have special features to live in rivers.

How do plants live in rivers?

Water lilies have roots at the bottom of the river to keep them from floating away.

Their leaves float on water so they can take in sunlight. Plants use sunlight to make food.

Bladderworts do not have any roots or leaves. They have small airless bags under water that help them catch food.

The bags trap tiny animals for the bladderworts to feed on.

Plants are very important for river **habitats**. They provide food and **shelter** for many animals.

Many plants provide a home for small animals.
These plants are called **microhabitats**.
A microhabitat is a very small habitat
within a larger habitat.

How do animals feed in rivers?

Crayfish eat plants and small animals.

The crayfish have large front **pincers** to grab and hold food. Smaller pincers on their legs help to tear away food and bring it to their mouths.

Catfish feed on plants, insects and small fish. They live on the bottoms of rivers where it is hard to see.

Catfish have whiskers called **barbels** that help them taste food before they put it in their mouths.

Dragonflies feed on other insects. Their large eyes allow them to see in every direction.

A dragonfly's four wings help it to move quickly in the air. It can catch other flying insects.

Kingfishers feed on fish and insects.

Their long, narrow beaks help them dive into water and catch fish.

How do animals hide in rivers?

Crocodiles are **predators**. They eat other animals for food.

A crocodile's eyes, ears and nostrils are high on its head so it can sneak up on **prey** without being seen.

Freshwater mussels are food to many animals.
Their green and brown shells help them to hide from predators.

How do animals move around in rivers?

A platypus uses its webbed front feet to paddle through water.

Its flat tail helps it steer.

Pond skaters live on the surface of rivers.

Thick hairs on a pond skater's legs keep it from sinking into the water.

How do animals survive under water?

Most fish use their **gills** to breathe under water.

Many other animals hold their breath and return to the surface to breathe.

gills (inside)

Diving bell spiders have a special way of breathing under water.

They make a bubble out of their own web and fill it with air.

How do animal babies survive in rivers?

Beavers build nests out of twigs, branches and leaves. They bite through wood with their large front teeth.

Beavers' nests, called lodges, provide safety and **shelter** for their young.

Caddisflies lay their eggs in water.

Some caddisfly babies make cases to protect their soft bodies as they grow.

That's amazing!

The alligator snapping turtle has a piece of flesh on its tongue that looks like a worm. Fish think it is food and swim right into its mouth.

Picture glossary

 **barbels** pointy body parts around the mouth of some fish. Barbels are used to feel and taste food.

 **gills** body parts of a fish that help it breathe

 **habitat** a place where an animal or plant lives

 **microhabitat** a very small habitat within a larger habitat

 **pincers** large front claws that are used to hold things

 **predator** an animal that hunts other animals for food

 **prey** an animal that is hunted by other animals for food

 **shelter** a place that protects from danger or bad weather

Find out more

Books

Ganeri, Anita. *Exploring Rivers: A Benjamin Blog and His Inquisitive Dog Investigation.* (Raintree, 2014)

Waldron, Melanie. *Rivers.* (Raintree, 2013)

Websites

http://kids.nationalgeographic.co.uk/kids/animals/creaturefeature
Under "Habitats" click "Freshwater" to see more pictures and information on river animals.

www.wildlifewatch.org.uk/explore-wildlife/habitats
Click "Freshwater and wet places" to search more plants and animals in river habitats.

Index

alligator snapping turtles 22
beavers 20
bladderworts 7
caddisflies 21
catfish 11
crayfish 10
crocodiles 14

diving bell spiders 19
dragonflies 12
freshwater mussels 15
kingfishers 13
platypuses 16
pond skaters 17
water lilies 6

Hairdresser

JAMES NIXON

PHOTOGRAPHY BY BOBBY HUMPHREY

W

This edition 2014

Copyright © Franklin Watts 2012, 2014
Franklin Watts
338 Euston Road
London NW1 3BH

Franklin Watts Australia
Level 17/207 Kent Street
Sydney, NSW 2000

Planning and production by
Discovery Books Limited
Editor: James Nixon
Design: sprout.uk.com
Commissioned photography: Bobby Humphrey

Dewey number: 646.7'24

ISBN: 978 1 4451 2946 4

Printed in China

Franklin Watts is a division of Hachette
Children's Books, an Hachette UK company.

www.hachette.co.uk

Acknowledgements: Shutterstock Images: p. 23
top (Losevsky Pavel).

The author, packager and publisher would like
to thank Remedy Hairdressing, Leeds, for their
help and participation in this book.

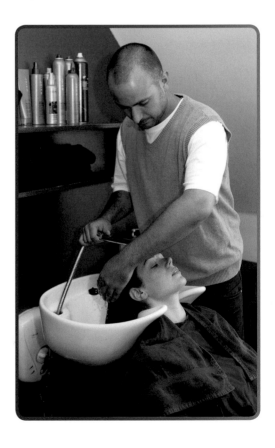

what we do

CONTENTS

4 I AM A HAIRDRESSER

6 GREETING CUSTOMERS

8 CHOOSING A STYLE

10 CUTTING HAIR

12 SHAPING THE HAIR

14 GAINING EXPERIENCE

16 COLOURING HAIR

18 USING PRODUCTS

20 HAIR CARE

22 GETTING ON

24 GLOSSARY

24 INDEX

Words in **bold** appear in the glossary on page 24.

I AM A HAIRDRESSER

My name is Hayley. I work as a stylist in a hairdresser's. This is our salon (right). The men have their hair cut downstairs. The women's section is upstairs. I cut and style both men's and women's hair.

The hairdressers in the salon work as a team to make sure the customers are looked after properly. The work is tiring. I spend most of the day on my feet, moving around different parts of the salon, washing, drying and styling hair.

▼ We use a range of techniques to provide customers with the shape, colour and **texture** of hair that they want.

There are a variety of brushes, scissors, products and other tools that I use to create different haircuts. Every customer's hair is different, but hairdressers know what styles and products are best for each person.

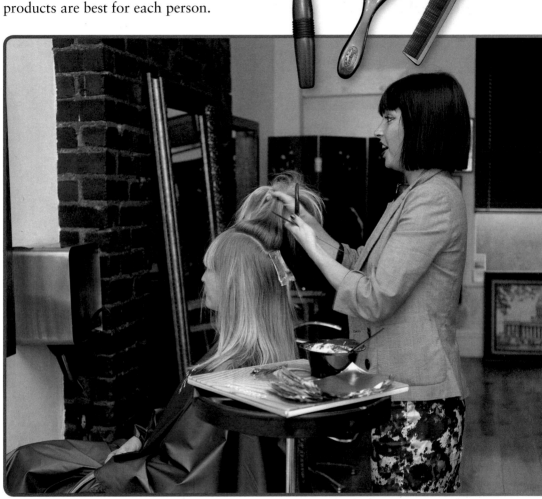

▲ *Chatting with the customers is a fun part of hairdressing.*

As a hairdresser it is important to form good relationships with your customers. You need to be friendly and chatty. My favourite part of the job is making people look good and feel happy about themselves.

KEY SKILLS

STAMINA – Even if you are tired and the salon is busy, you must be enthusiastic towards customers and do a neat job.

5

GREETING CUSTOMERS

▲ *We help customers with their coats and bags and find a place for them to sit and wait.*

Making customers feel comfortable while they are in the salon is as important as the haircut itself. When a customer arrives you need to give them a warm welcome.

Hairdressers must make sure that customers do not have to wait for long. Keeping the customers happy and satisfied will mean they come back to have their hair cut time and time again.

KEY SKILLS

FRIENDLY AND OUTGOING – You need to have good people skills and the ability to put customers at ease. Many customers will want to have a chat.

When I am ready, I take a customer to a chair in front of a mirror and ask them what they want from their **appointment**. Do they want a simple trim or a full restyle? I have to listen well so I know exactly what they are looking for. Then I know that they will be happy with the end result.

▶ *During the consultation I find out what style will suit the customer best.*

At the reception desk I take payments and answer the telephone (left). Some customers ring up to book an appointment in advance. I write the time and date down in the book and whether they want a cut, colour or restyle. We will then make sure that there is a stylist available at that time.

CHOOSING A STYLE

Hairdressers give expert advice to customers when they are choosing a hairstyle. Sometimes I suggest ideas that the customer has never tried before. I choose styles and colours (right) that I think will suit the customer's type of hair and face shape.

Once a style is chosen, we wash the customer's hair at the basin. First, we test that the water is the right temperature. Then we cleanse the hair with shampoo by massaging it all the way through to the roots.

TOOLS OF THE TRADE

There are lots of different shampoos for different hair types. A shampoo for dry hair leaves an oily coating on the hair. If someone has greasy hair we use a shampoo that contains fewer oils.

KEY SKILLS

CREATIVITY – Hairdressers should be naturally creative and able to visualise if a change of hairstyle will suit the customer.

This is my colleague Nick (right) rinsing shampoo out before he conditions the hair to make it soft and shiny. **Conditioner** is rubbed into the tips of the hair, and then this is rinsed out as well.

Now the hair is ready to be cut. The customer is wrapped in a gown and a rubber collar is placed at the back of the neck, so they do not get covered in hair.

▼ *Nick places the rubber collar on to the customer's neck.*

CUTTING HAIR

Hairdressers use a variety of cutting techniques to create different hairstyles. A simple haircut called a bob is the same length all over. Layered hair is cut at different lengths overlapping each other.

A short back and sides is a popular style among men. To cut the top and sides we use a technique called club cutting. With club cutting, a section of hair is held out from the head and cut off at the tips (right). The sides are cut as short as possible and then this is merged to the top which is left a bit longer.

▼ *At the back of the head and around the ears, the hair is too short for a finger guide, so the scissors are used over a comb.*

KEY SKILLS

ATTENTION TO DETAIL –
You need to have a steady hand
and be very precise.

To neaten up the hairline at the top
of the neck and above the ear I use
the **clippers** (above) and the scissors
freehand (right).

Then to give the longer hair on
top some spikes or texture, I cut
it to different lengths by pointing
the scissors vertically over the
comb (below).

▶ *I always check that the customer is happy
with the result. They can see the back of their
head when I hold the mirror up.*

11

SHAPING THE HAIR

After the hair is cut, hairdressers blow-dry it into shape and use products to hold the hair in place. This is like the icing on the cake.

While drying, the hairdresser breaks the hair up with their fingers and angles it in the right direction. Then the hair is dried with special brushes to leave a smooth finish.

▲ *Nick uses an electric hand dryer in combination with a round brush.*

TOOLS OF THE TRADE

Round brush – To give hair extra lift, a round brush can be used while drying.

Vent brush – Hot air flows through the holes of this brush (right) to give shorter hair texture.

Diffuser – To dry long, wavy hair, a hair dryer attachment, called a diffuser, is used.

Once the hair is dry I can use electrical curling tongs to create waves or hair straighteners to remove unwanted curls. As a finishing touch I use hairspray to hold the hair in place. Sometimes I rub wax or gel evenly through the hair and pull it into shape.

▶ *Hair can be wrapped around straightening irons to produce neat curls.*

▼ *When I apply the hairspray I protect the customer's face with my hand.*

KEY SKILLS

PRESENTATION – In the beauty industry it is important to look good and keep yourself well groomed. The customers will then be confident that you will do a good job.

▶ *By rubbing wax into the hair I can create a spiky style that holds in place.*

GAINING EXPERIENCE

Trainee stylists learn the skills of hairdressing on the job. While they work, trainees also attend college to gain their professional **qualifications**.

This is our trainee, Miles (left). When a trainee position came up at the salon a friend told him about it. He had never considered hairdressing before but decided it was the right job for him. Miles goes to college once a week to do his National Vocational Qualifications (NVQs) in hairdressing. He has been here a year and in another year's time he will be fully qualified.

▶ Miles sweeps the hair up when the customers leave.

In the salon, trainees play an important part in looking after the customers as they arrive and wait. They also make sure that the salon is always kept clean and tidy. Miles is responsible for sorting out the fresh towels (right) and gowns. They need to be washed after each use.

Trainees assist stylists by carrying out less complicated jobs, such as washing customers' hair. They also observe and learn from the stylists at work.

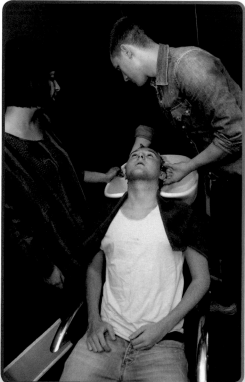

If you are applying for a trainee job it is useful to have some experience of dealing with the public, such as working in a shop. Good GCSEs in English and Maths, as well as Art to show your creativity, will also give you an advantage.

◄ *I help the trainees to learn. Here, I am making sure Miles washes the customer's hair correctly.*

KEY SKILLS

TEAMWORK – In a busy salon you need to work as part of a team.

COLOURING HAIR

Colouring hair requires advanced skills. You must understand how to use **tints** correctly to achieve the shade you want. You must also know how to work safely with **chemical** products.

▲ *Colour books*

I show customers a colour book to help them select a shade, and give them recommendations based on their natural hair colour. They can choose a permanent hair colour or a temporary colour that will come out when the hair is washed. Temporary colour **mousses** are scrunched into the hair using rubber gloves.

KEY SKILLS

FASHION CONSCIOUS – You need to have a keen sense of style and you need to keep up to date with the latest looks and trends.

When permanently coloured hair grows, the roots need redoing. This is Gerry (left). He is pasting tint on to a customer's roots with a brush. The tint is left on for 45 minutes and then rinsed off.

Bleach is used to lighten the colour of hair. Because bleach can be damaging to the hair we often use a highlighting technique. With highlights, only some strands of the hair are coloured. I weave the strands of hair with a tail comb (below). Then I rest the hair on top of tinfoil and apply the tint with the brush (right).

TOOLS OF THE TRADE

When I have finished applying the colour, I sit customers under a special **infrared** heater to help the colour **penetrate** the hair.

USING PRODUCTS

Hairdressers need an understanding of a huge variety of products. Once stylists are qualified they continue to build up their knowledge and stay aware of new products on the market.

Sometimes hairdressers attend short courses that introduce them to new products. The kinds of products available are changing all the time. Sales **reps** often pop in and talk to us about new items. It is important that we use and store products correctly.

▲ *Colours and* **peroxides** *have to be stored in a room where the temperature is cool.*

The chemicals in hair products mean that if you have skin problems, hairdressing may not be a suitable job for you. When a customer is having a tint for the first time I check that they will not have an **allergic reaction** to the product. I do this by testing a tiny amount on the inside of their elbow the day before their appointment.

Hairdressers must know which products can improve the look of different types of hair. For example, for fine hair, a stylist may use a dry mousse to give the hair extra **volume**. Here, Nick is working a gloopy, smoothing balm into the customer's hair to strengthen it (right).

▼ *Smoothing balms like this one make the hair strong and stop thick hair going frizzy.*

KEY SKILLS

OPENNESS TO NEW IDEAS AND TECHNIQUES – Hairdressers continue to expand their skills and knowledge throughout their careers.

REDKEN

outshine 01

19

HAIR CARE

Hairdressing is also about helping customers keep their hair healthy. I give customers advice on how to treat any hair or scalp conditions they may have.

Before I cut hair I always analyse the customer's hair and scalp. I check for any hair problems that might need attention, such as **split ends** or **beaded hair**. For some scalp conditions, such as **psoriasis,** I might advise the customer to use a different shampoo. I also keep an eye out for any infections or **lice infestations**.

Hygiene is important so that infections are not passed on between customers. Brushes and combs are scrubbed to get the hair off and dipped into a disinfectant, called Barbicide, after every use (right).

▲ *I check the hair and scalp with a comb and keep an eye out for any lice.*

KEY SKILLS

GOOD COMMUNICATION – You need to be clear so that customers understand your advice.

◀ *Before every cut I wash my hands and rinse the Barbicide off the combs.*

There are certain hairstyling techniques where you have to be very careful not to seriously damage the hair. For example, putting in **hair extensions** is a delicate job that takes time. Small sections of hair are glued in with a sponge strip.

▼ *Hair extensions can transform a customer's appearance, but I must be careful that the glue does not damage the health of the hair.*

▲ *I advise my customers how to look after their hair extensions. If they brush their hair incorrectly they could fall out!*

GETTING ON

To become a qualified hairdresser you need to do *Level 1 and 2 NVQs in Hairdressing. Level 1* covers basic work, such as health and safety and shampooing. *Level 2* introduces you to cutting and colouring techniques.

Here is my *Level 2* certificate (left). You can get your qualifications at college and then look for a job, or you can try to find work straight away as an **apprentice**. I was working as a waitress when I decided I wanted to be a hairdresser. Every night after work I popped into three or four salons and asked for an apprenticeship. By the end of the week a salon had offered me a job!

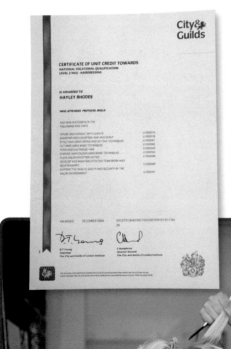

City&
Guilds

CERTIFICATE OF UNIT CREDIT TOWARDS
NATIONAL VOCATIONAL QUALIFICATION
LEVEL 2 NVQ - HAIRDRESSING

IS AWARDED TO
HAYLEY RHODES

Hairdressers can find work in places other than salons. Hospitals, care homes, army bases and even cruise ships employ stylists. With experience you can progress to be a senior stylist or salon manager. *NVQ Levels 3 and 4* provide you with the skills to become a salon manager. Stylists can choose to become self-employed and open their own salon or work from home. Then they can work the hours that suit them. Top hairdressers can even go on to become stylists for celebrities or catwalk models (left)!

There are also opportunites for hairdressers to become expert in one particular area. For example, you could become a colour technician specialising in dyes. Some hairdressers go on to train as scalp problem experts while others become wig makers and fitters.

◀ *Hairdressers continually update their skills so that they can offer the latest styles.*

GLOSSARY

allergic reaction A damaging response by the body when it comes into contact with a substance.

appointment An arrangement to be somewhere at a particular time.

apprentice A trainee who learns the skills of the job as they work.

beaded hair Short, fragile, broken hair.

bleach A chemical used to make a material become white or much lighter.

chemical A substance used in chemistry, which can be damaging to the skin.

clippers An electrical device for trimming hair.

conditioner A liquid applied to the hair to improve its condition.

freehand Without the aid of a guide.

hair extensions Strands of hair attached to a person's own hair to make it longer.

hygiene The practice of keeping yourself and your surroundings clean.

infestation The presence of something unwanted, in large numbers.

infrared A wave of light that is not visible to the human eye.

lice Wingless insects that infest the hair of humans.

mousse A light, foamy product that is applied to hair so it can be styled more easily.

penetrate To get deep into something.

peroxide A chemical mixture used as a bleach for the hair.

psoriasis A skin disease marked by red, itchy, scaly patches.

qualification A pass of a course or exam to show you are skilled at a particular job or activity.

rep A salesperson acting on behalf of a company.

split ends The tips of a person's hair which are split and damaged.

texture The feel and appearance of the surface of the hair.

tint A dye for colouring the hair.

volume Thickness of a person's hair.

INDEX

appointments 7, 19

bleaches 17
brushes 5, 12, 16, 17, 20

chatting 5, 6
chemicals 16, 19
clippers 11
club cutting 10
colours 4, 7, 8, 16–17, 18, 22, 23
combs 10, 17, 20
conditioners 9
curling tongs 13
cutting hair 4, 6, 7, 9, 10–11, 20, 22

diffusers 12
drying 4, 12

gels 13

hair straighteners 13
hair types 8, 19
hairspray 13
highlights 17
hygiene 20

lice 20

mirrors 7, 11
mousses 16, 19

products 5, 12, 16, 18–19

qualifications 14, 22, 23

reception 7

salon 4, 5, 6, 14, 15, 22, 23
scalp 20, 23
scissors 5, 10, 11
shampoos 8, 9, 20, 22
split ends 20
styles 5, 7, 8–9, 10, 16, 23

textures 4, 11, 12
tints 16, 17, 19
trainees 14, 15

washing 4, 8, 15, 16
waxes 13